Famous & Fun Rock

9 Appealing Piano Arrangements

Carol Matz

Famous & Fun Rock, Book 4, contains 9 carefully selected popular rock hits. Each piece has been arranged especially for early intermediate pianists, yet remains faithful to the sound of the original. The arrangements can be used as a supplement to any method. Book 4 includes swing rhythm, 6/8 time, and key signatures with no more than one sharp or flat.

Carol Matz

Produced by
Alfred Music
P.O. Box 10003
Van Nuys, CA 91410-0003
alfred.com

Printed in USA.

ISBN-10: 0-7390-9606-0
ISBN-13: 978-0-7390-9606-2

Great Balls of Fire

Words and Music by
Otis Blackwell and Jack Hammer
Arranged by Carol Matz

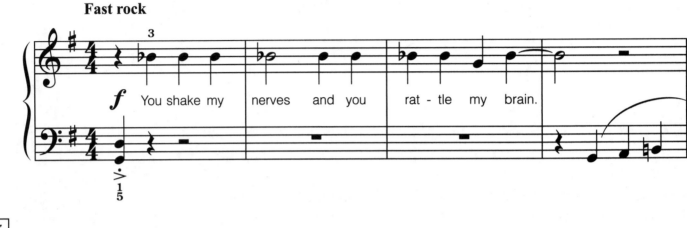

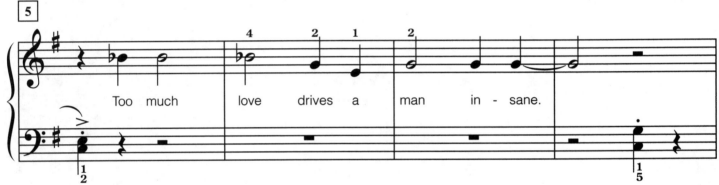

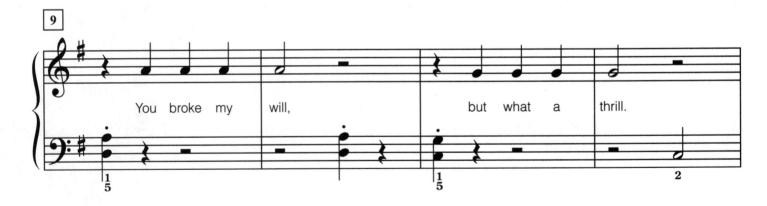

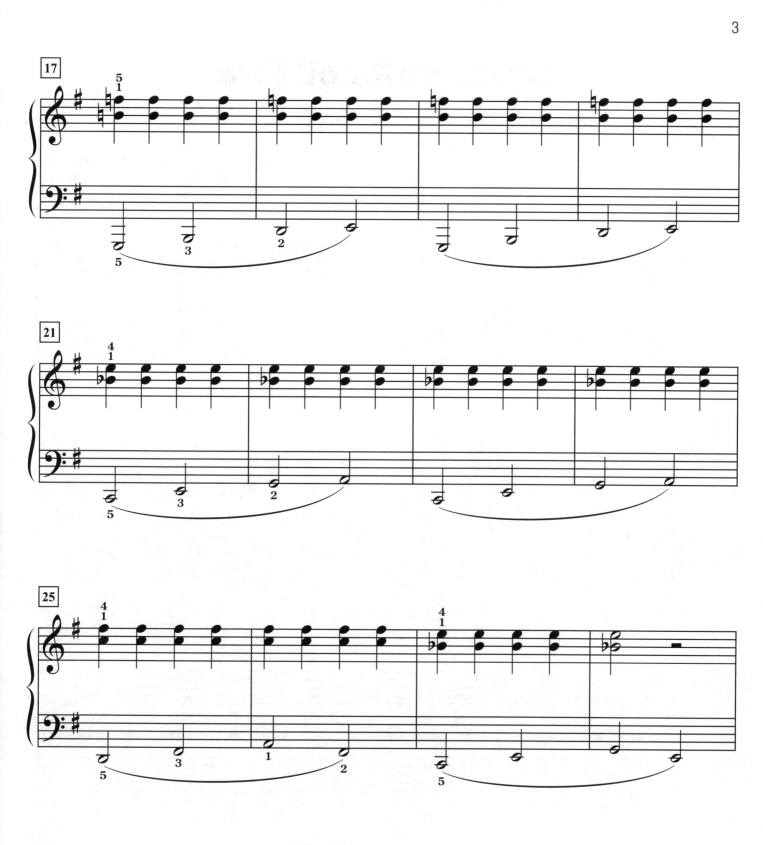

Good - ness gra - cious, great balls of fire!

8va

(We're Gonna)
Rock Around the Clock

Words and Music by
Max C. Freedman and Jimmy De Knight
Arranged by Carol Matz

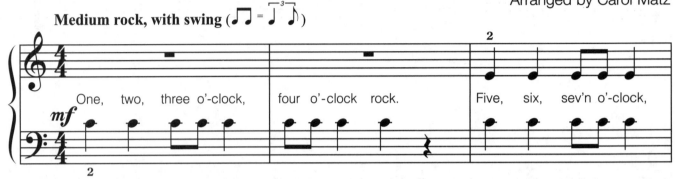

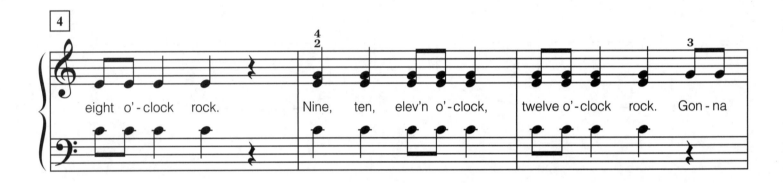

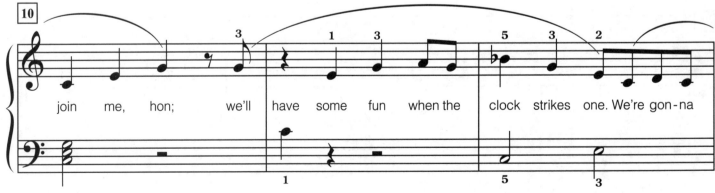

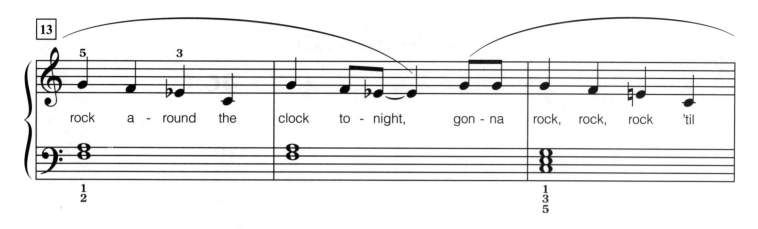

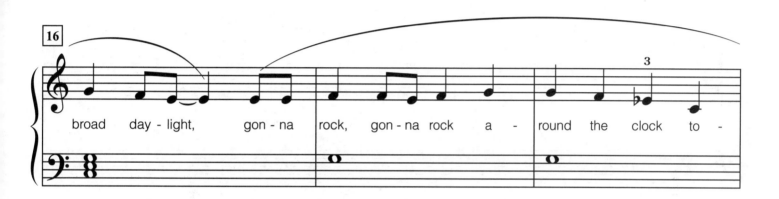

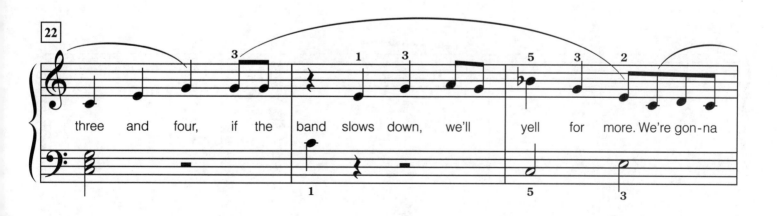

6

rock a - round the clock to - night, gon - na rock, rock, rock 'til

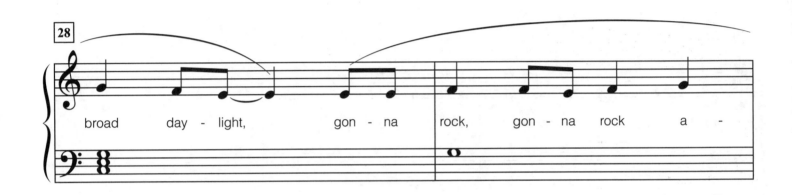

broad day - light, gon - na rock, gon - na rock a -

round the clock to - night!

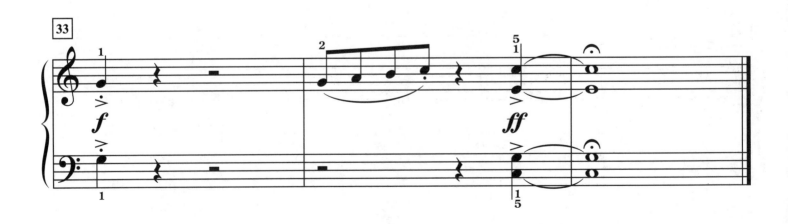

It's My Party

Words and Music by
Herb Wiener, John Gluck and Wally Gold
Arranged by Carol Matz

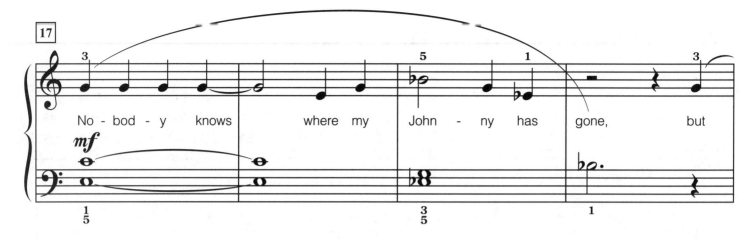

17

No - bod - y knows where my John - ny has gone, but

mf

21

Ju - dy left the same time.

25

Why was he hold - ing her hand when

29

he's sup - posed to be mine?

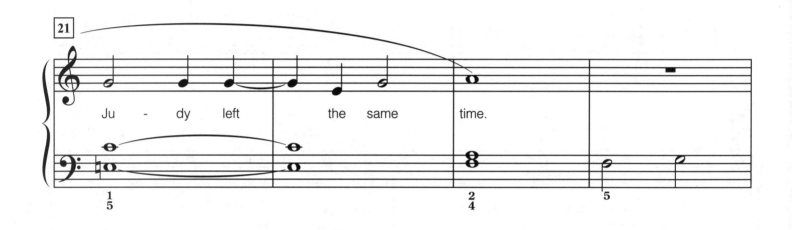

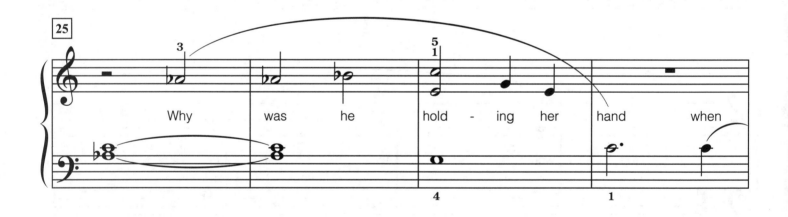

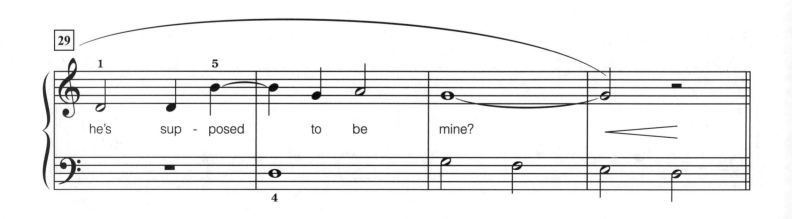

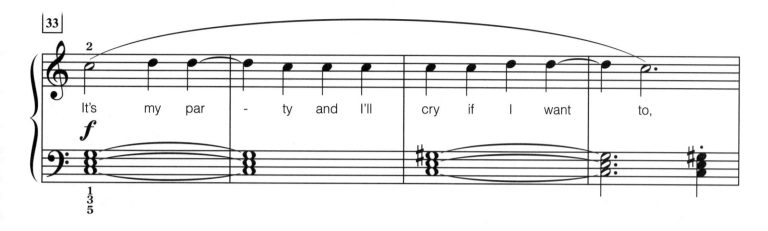

It's my par - ty and I'll cry if I want to,

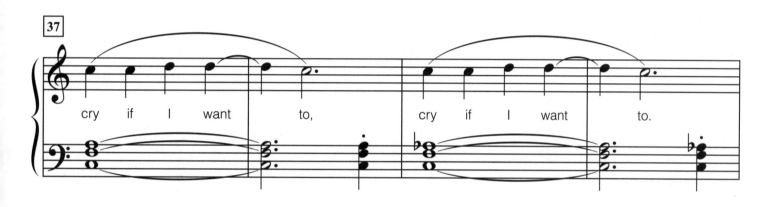

cry if I want to, cry if I want to.

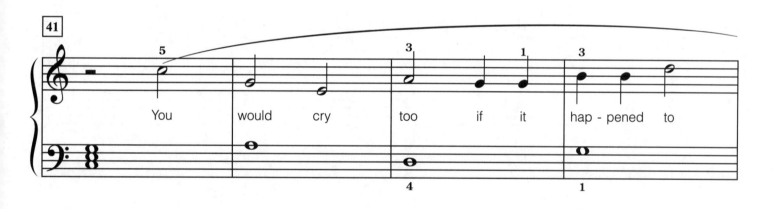

You would cry too if it hap - pened to

you.

Aquarius

(from *Hair*)

Lyrics by James Rado and Gerome Ragni
Music by Galt Macdermot
Arranged by Carol Matz

Moderately fast

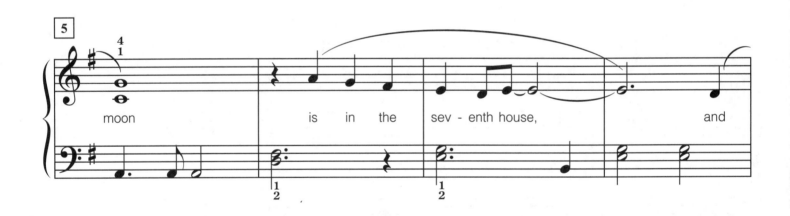

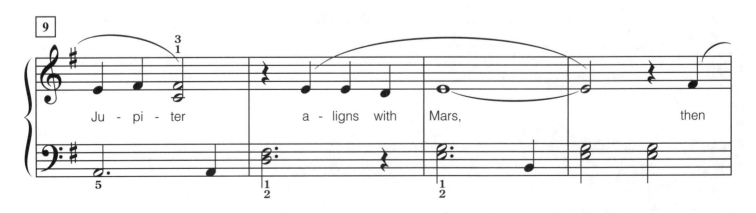

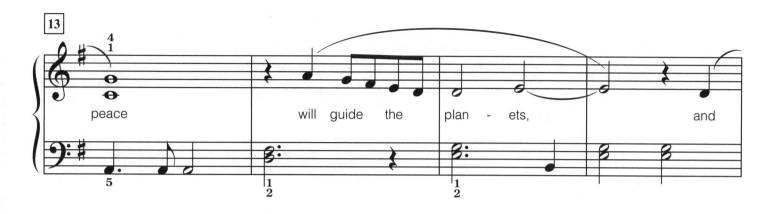

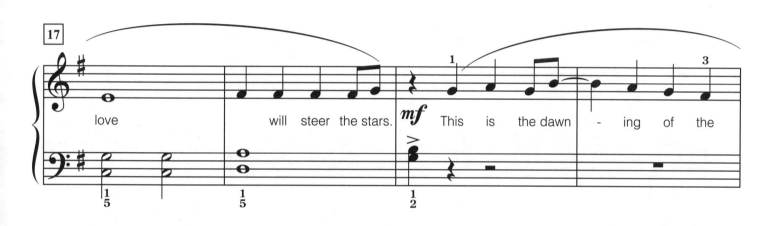

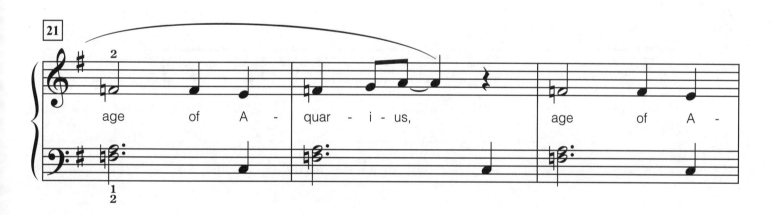

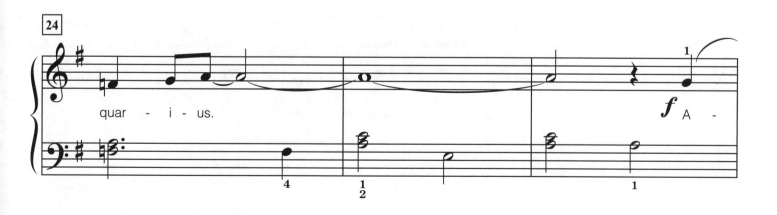

12

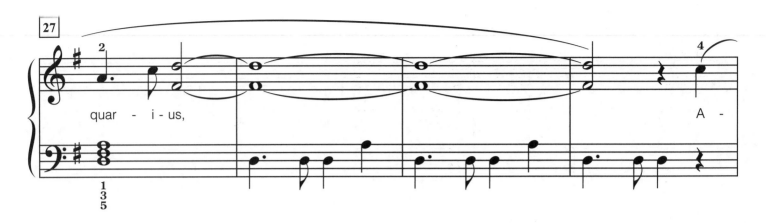

quar - i - us,   A -

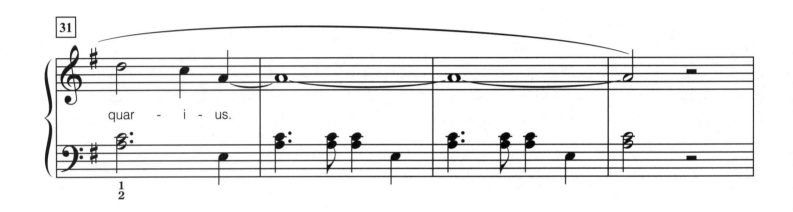

quar - i - us.

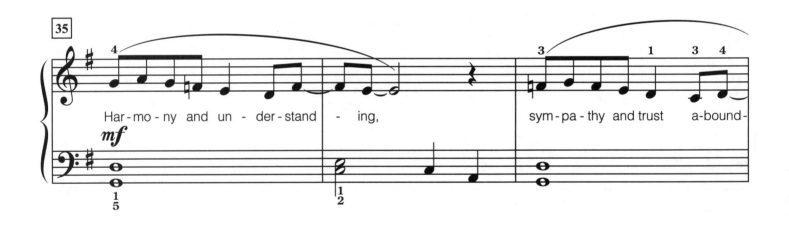

Har - mo - ny and un - der - stand - ing,   sym - pa - thy and trust a - bound -

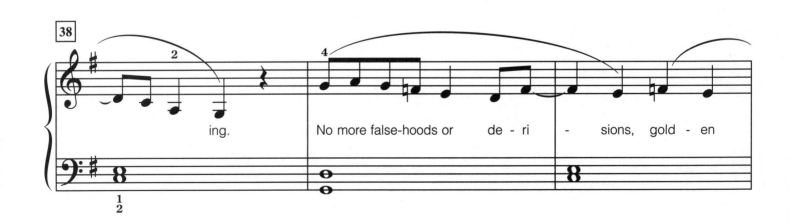

ing.   No more false-hoods or de - ri - sions, gold - en

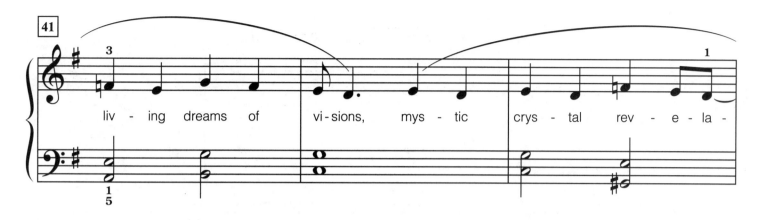

liv - ing dreams of vi - sions, mys - tic crys - tal rev - e - la -

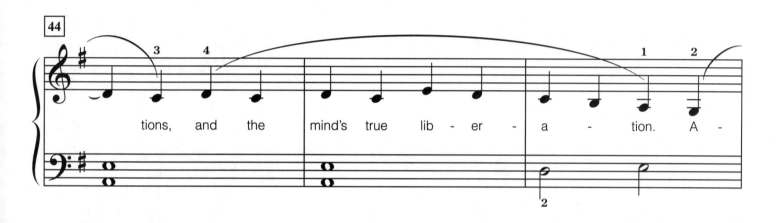

tions, and the mind's true lib - er - a - tion. A -

quar - i - us, *cresc.* A -

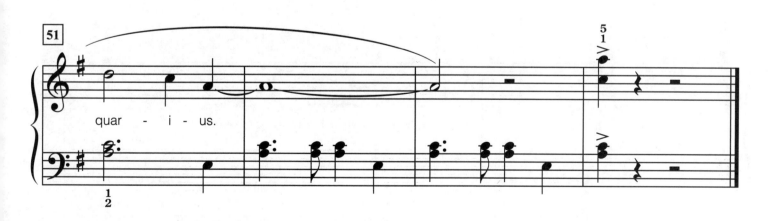

quar - i - us.

The Sound of Silence

Words and Music by Paul Simon
Arranged by Carol Matz

Moderately slow

Hel-lo, dark-ness, my old friend,

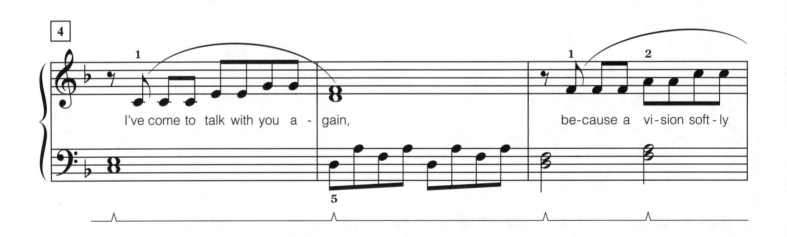

I've come to talk with you a - gain,   be-cause a vi - sion soft - ly

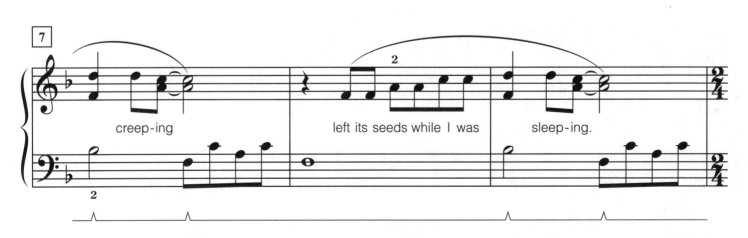

creep-ing   left its seeds while I was   sleep-ing.

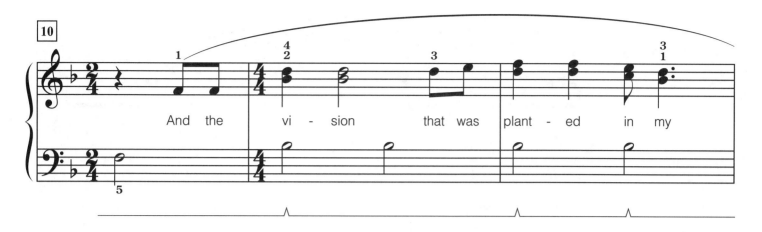

And the vi - sion that was plant - ed in my

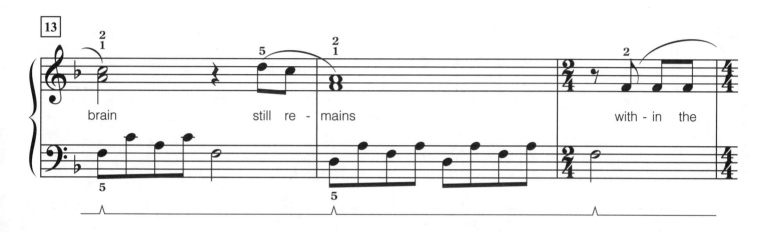

brain still re - mains with - in the

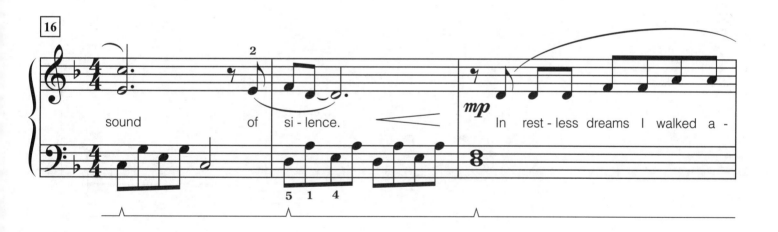

sound of si - lence. *mp* In rest - less dreams I walked a -

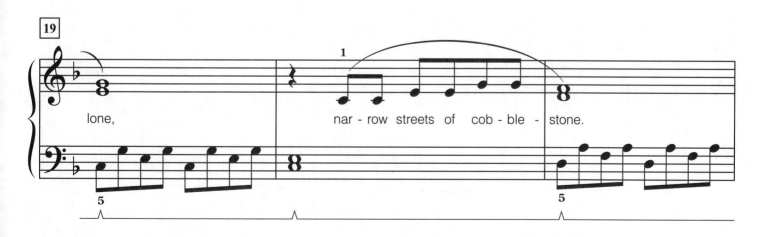

lone, nar - row streets of cob - ble - stone.

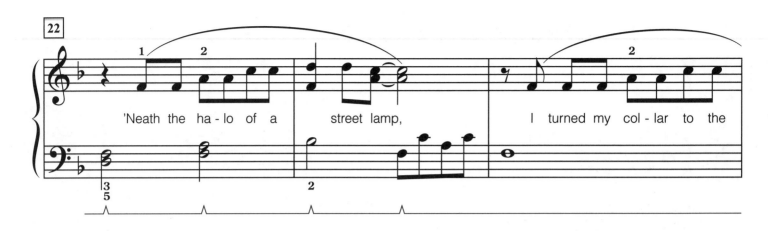

'Neath the ha - lo of a street lamp, I turned my col - lar to the

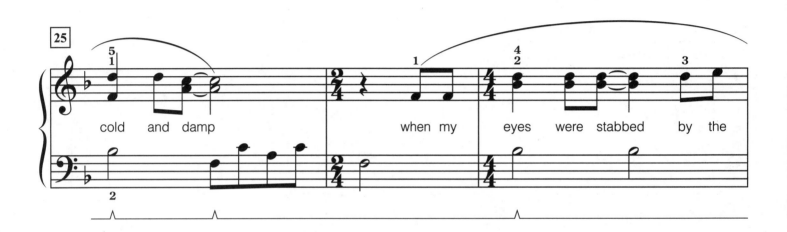

cold and damp when my eyes were stabbed by the

flash of a ne - on light that split the night

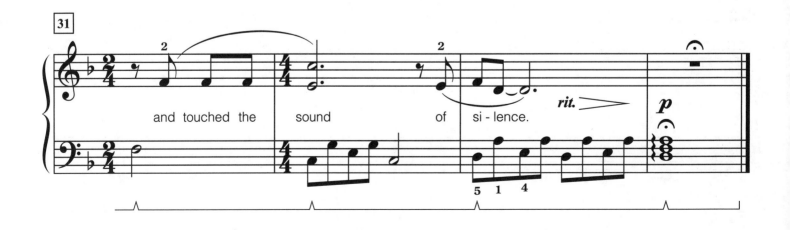

and touched the sound of si - lence.

rit.

Boulevard of Broken Dreams

Words by Billie Joe
Music by Green Day
Arranged by Carol Matz

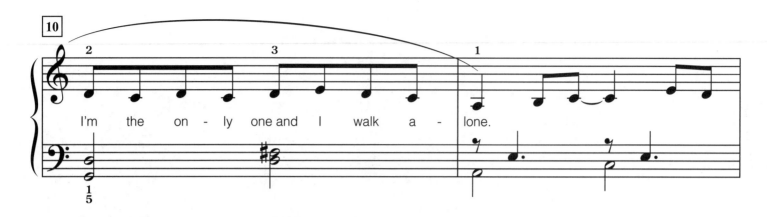

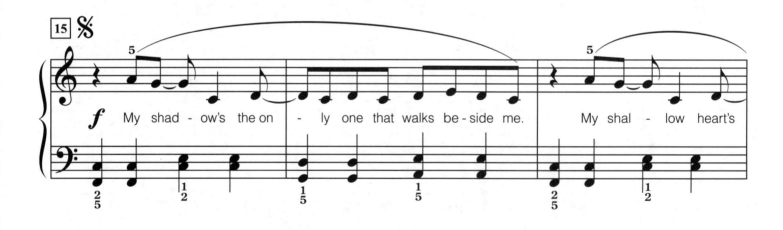

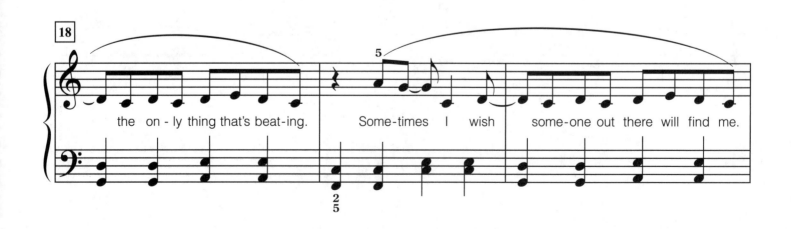

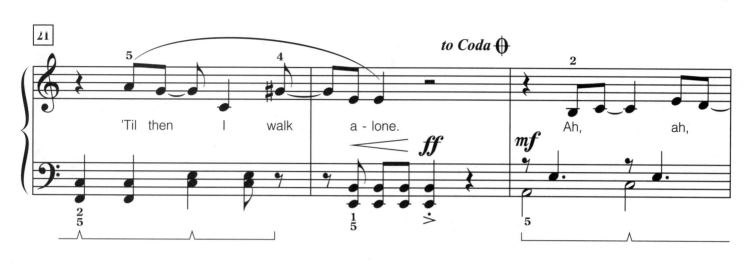

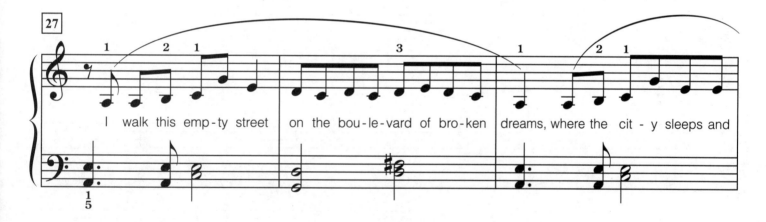

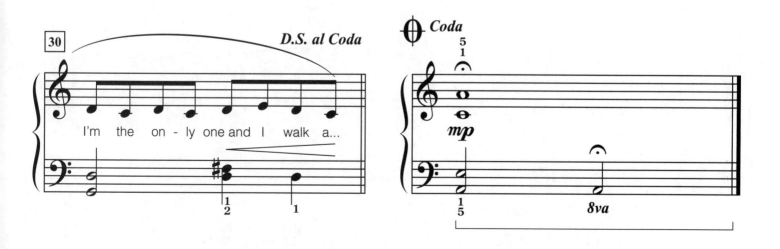

Bye Bye Love

Words and Music by
Boudleaux Bryant and Felice Bryant
Arranged by Carol Matz

hel - lo emp - ti - ness; I feel like I could die.

Bye bye, my love, good - bye.

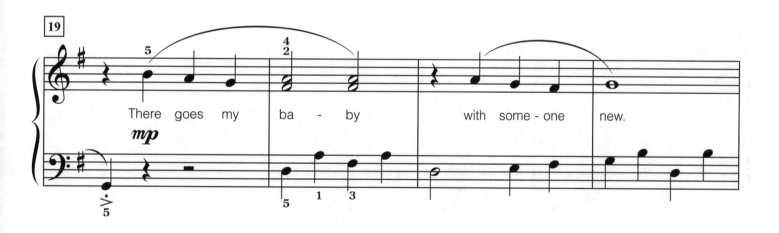

There goes my ba - by with some - one new.

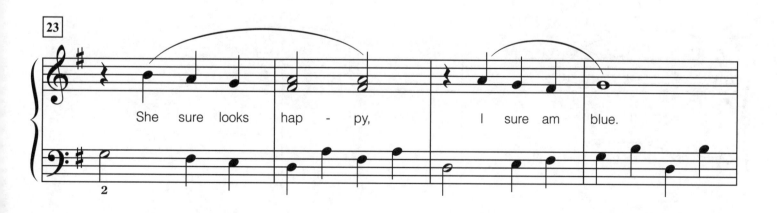

She sure looks hap - py, I sure am blue.

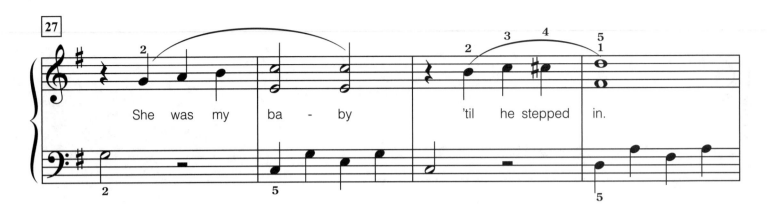

She was my ba - by 'til he stepped in.

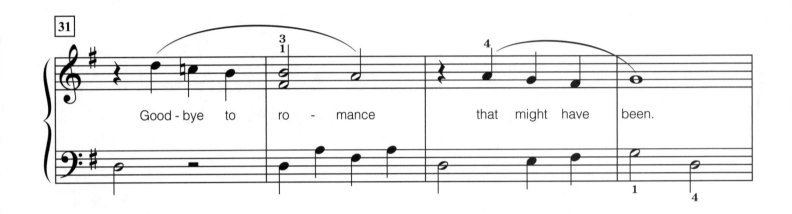

Good - bye to ro - mance that might have been.

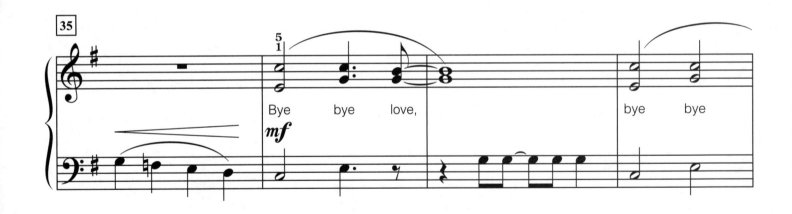

Bye bye love, bye bye

mf

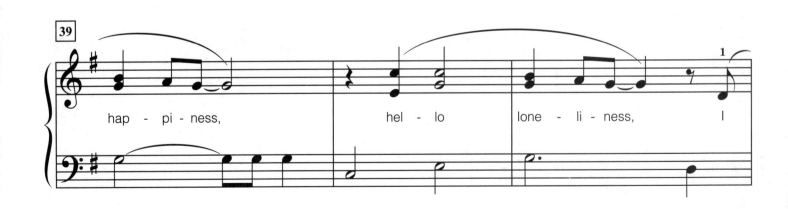

hap - pi - ness, hel - lo lone - li - ness, I

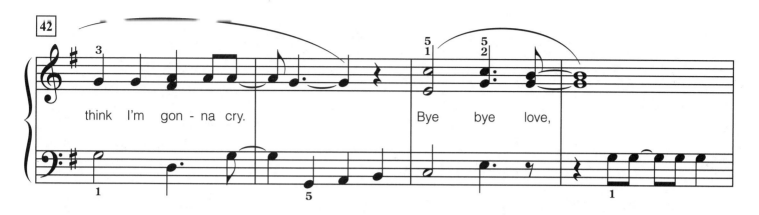

think I'm gon - na cry.　　　　　Bye　bye　love,

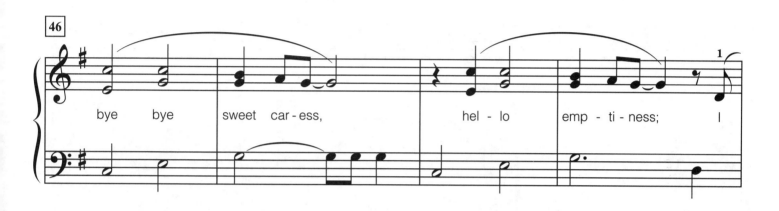

bye　bye　sweet car - ess,　　　　hel - lo　emp - ti - ness;　　I

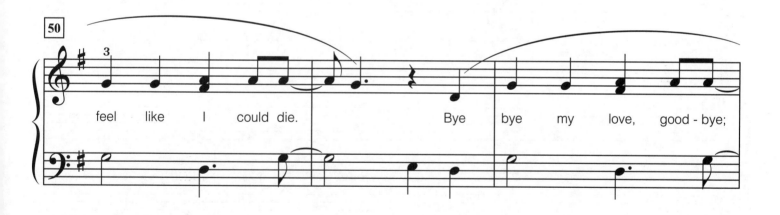

feel　like　I　could die.　　　　Bye　bye　my　love,　good - bye;

good - bye,　my　love,　good - bye.　　　　　　　　　f

I Got You Babe

Words and Music by Sonny Bono
Arranged by Carol Matz

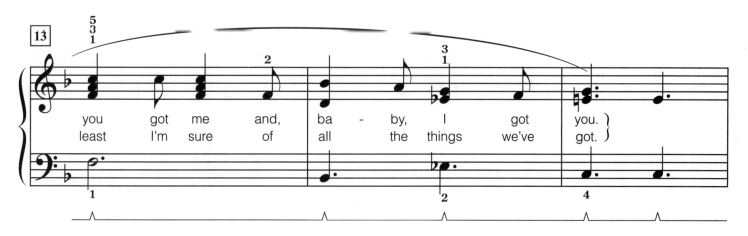

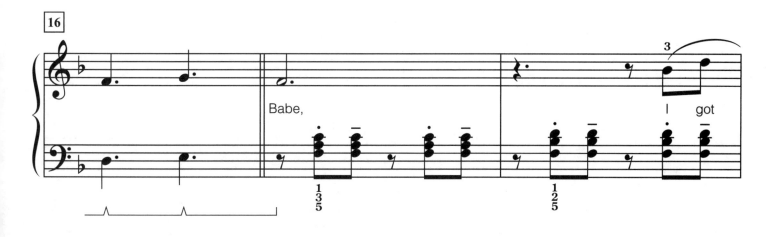

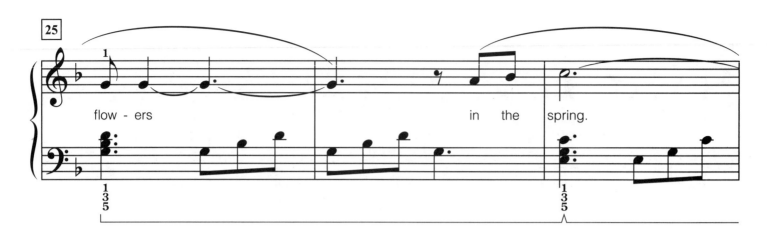

flow - ers   in the spring.

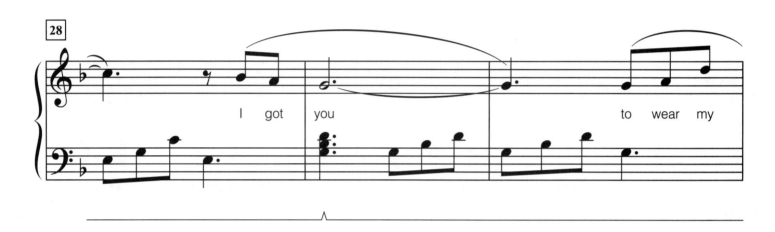

I got you   to wear my

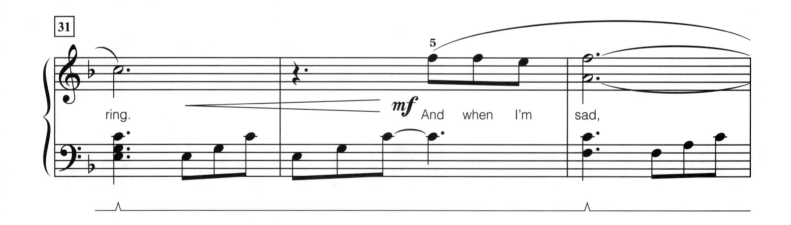

ring.   mf And when I'm   sad,

you're   a   clown,   and if I get

Hey There Delilah

Words and Music by Tom Higgenson
Arranged by Carol Matz

Moderately

mp Hey there, De - li - lah, what's it like in New York Cit - y? I'm a

thou - sand miles a - way but, girl, to - night you look so pret - ty, yes, you

do. Times Square can't shine as bright as you. I swear it's

true. Hey there, De - li - lah, don't you worry a - bout the dis - tance, I'm right

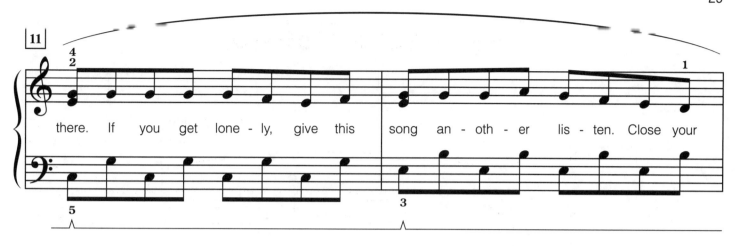

there. If you get lone-ly, give this song an - oth - er lis - ten. Close your

eyes. Listen to my voice, it's my dis - guise. I'm by your

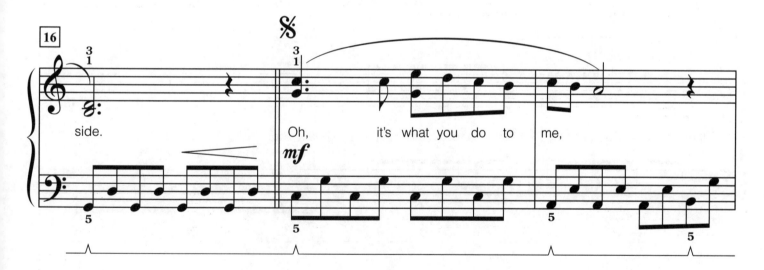

side. Oh, it's what you do to me,

oh, it's what you do to me. Oh, it's what you do to

to Coda ⊕

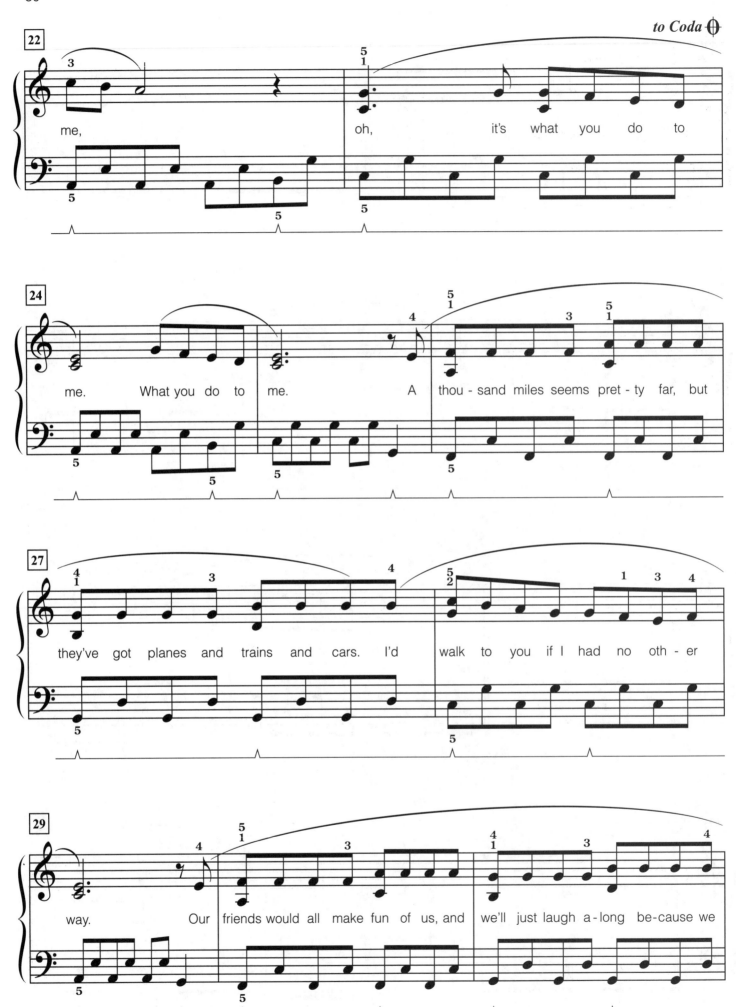

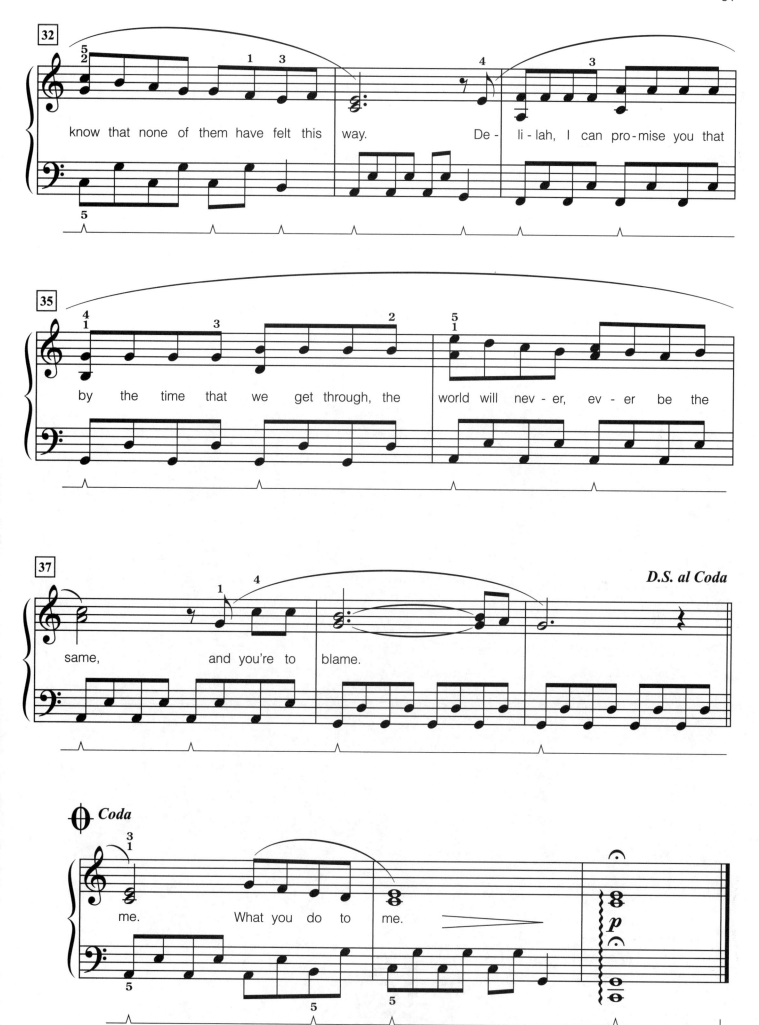

Famous & Fun series
Christmas • Classics • Favorites • Pop • Pop Duets

Famous & Fun Pop Duets from the Famous & Fun series provide valuable supplementary material that has been carefully selected for student appeal. These effective and enjoyable arrangements can supplement any piano method and provide motivating recital material.

Highlights of the Famous & Fun series:
- carefully selected pieces
- well-graded arrangements
- levels remain consistent throughout the series
- musical, motivating arrangements

Carol Matz is an active composer, arranger, author and editor of educational piano materials. She also maintains a piano studio where she enjoys teaching students of all ages and abilities.

Carol studied composition, arranging and orchestration at the University of Miami, with an emphasis on studio and jazz writing. In addition to her compositions and arrangements for piano, Carol has written for a variety of ensembles including orchestra, jazz big band and string quartet. Her work also includes studio arrangements and recording sessions for a number of artists in Miami-area recording studios. Carol serves as a keyboard editor for Alfred.

Famous & Fun Pop Duets, Book 1
(27705)
(Early Elementary)

If I Only Had a Brain
Itsy Bitsy Teenie Weenie Yellow Polka Dot Bikini
The James Bond Theme
Mairzy Doats
(Meet) the Flintstones
The Rose
Yo Ho (A Pirate's Life for Me)

Famous & Fun Pop Duets, Book 2
(27706)
(Early Elementary to Elementary)

I'd Like to Teach the World to Sing
The Lion Sleeps Tonight
The Merry Old Land of Oz
The Siamese Cat Song
This Land Is Your Land
Wipe Out

Famous & Fun Pop Duets, Book 3
(27707)
(Elementary to Late Elementary)

Arabian Nights
The Ballad of Gilligan's Isle
Blue Moon
The Chicken Dance
Great Balls of Fire
The Imperial March

Famous & Fun Pop Duets, Book 4
(28985)
(Early Intermediate)

Chim Chim Cher-ee
Consider Yourself
Hakuna Matata
Itsy Bitsy Teenie Weenie Yellow Polka Dot Bikini
Music! Music! Music! (Put Another Nickel In)
The Pink Panther
Theme from New York, New York
We're Off to See the Wizard

Famous & Fun Pop Duets, Book 5
(28986)
(Intermediate)

Cruella De Vil
If I Only Had a Brain
The James Bond Theme
Star Wars (Main Title)
Superman Theme
You're the One That I Want

Alfred
alfred.com

ISBN-10: 0-7390-9606-0
ISBN-13: 978-0-7390-9606-2
50899
41005
9 780739 096062

The Virtuosic Performer

9 Exciting Late Elementary to Early Intermediate Piano Solos

Margaret Goldston

Book One

Alfred